Ten Poems about Music

THE YELLOW ALBUM

Candlestick Press

Published by:

Candlestick Press,
Diversity House, 72 Nottingham Road, Arnold, Nottingham NG5 6LF
www.candlestickpress.co.uk

Design and typesetting by Craig Twigg

Printed by Ratcliff & Roper Print Group, Nottinghamshire, UK

Selection and Introduction © Kim Moore, 2022

Cover illustration © Melissa Lhoirit, 2022
www.meliprints.com

Candlestick Press monogram © Barbara Shaw, 2008

© Candlestick Press, 2022

Donation to Our Dementia Choir
www.ourdementiachoir.com

ISBN 978 1 913627 11 9

Acknowledgements

The poems in this pamphlet are reprinted from the following books, all by
permission of the publishers listed unless stated otherwise. Every effort has been
made to trace the copyright holders of the poems published in this book. The
editor and publisher apologise if any material has been included without
permission or without the appropriate acknowledgement, and would be glad to be
told of anyone who has not been consulted.

Thanks are due to all the copyright holders cited below for their kind permission:

Abeer Ameer, *Inhale/Exile* (Seren Books, 2021). Jonathan Edwards, *Gen* (Seren
Books, 2018) by kind permission of the author. Carrie Etter, *Bad Lilies* online
magazine, by kind permission of the author https://www.badlilies.uk/carrie-etter.
WS Graham, *New Collected Poems* (Faber & Faber, 2004). Reproduced with
permission of the Estate of WS Graham. Copyright © the Estate of WS Graham,
2004. Hannah Lowe, *The Kids* (Bloodaxe Books, 2021) www.bloodaxebooks.com.
Faisal Mohyuddin, *The Displaced Children of Displaced Children* (Eyewear
Publishing, 2018). Kim Moore, poem first published in this anthology.

All permissions cleared courtesy of Suzanne Fairless-Aitken
c/o Swift Permissions swiftpermissions@gmail.com

Where poets are no longer living, their dates are given.

Contents

Introduction

In another life I was a musician. I went to music college and trained as a classical trumpet player and then worked for many years as a music teacher. After 'retiring' from playing due to performance anxiety, I've gradually started to make my way back towards music, starting to build practice back into my daily life and performing once again in orchestras, soul bands and brass bands.

Why are parents always right? They told me the trumpet would be waiting for me when I was ready to find it again, and so it was, and so it is, which is partly what my commissioned poem, 'The Trumpeter', explores. Call it a haunting or call it faithfulness, but I realised through writing this poem that I never really left music, or it never left me, that no matter how many times I turned away from it, I carried the trumpet with me.

Music is transformational, a place where the strangest change can happen. The speaker in Emily Dickinson's poem hears a church organ and *something* happens to her, although she doesn't quite understand what. In 'The Concert', Edna St Vincent Millay recounts a conversation between two lovers as one insists they will go to a concert alone, saying: "I will come back to you, I swear I will; / And you will know me still. / I shall be only a little taller / Than when I went."

Twelve years as a music teacher have left me with a soft spot for poems about teaching and learning. As well as the excellent 'Etudier' by Hannah Lowe, I've also chosen 'The Third Lesson' from WS Graham's 'Johann Joachim Quantz's Five Lessons'. The familiarity and love is shown both through encouragement and exasperation, but this poem illustrates perfectly the link between metaphor and magical teaching.

I'm delighted that this pamphlet is a literary duet with Cerys Matthews whose own selection of poems (*Ten Poems about Music: The Blue Album*) is an accompanying title. I hope you'll find that our selections speak to each other in interesting ways.

Kim Moore

The Pianist at The Grand

What are you but a head behind a desk?
Can't you do something, mister? You just sit there,
your foot busy on the accelerator,
but your long bonnet going slowly nowhere.
The hero of my poem's doing nothing,

nada. Your music is another matter.
At the end of your hands, a troop of gymnasts,
who want to twist and twirl, who want to whirl
and dance, to do some mischief in this world.
And look, my bobbing head just can't say *No*

to your left hand, while your right fingers solo,
get busy, crazy, get excited, go
apeshit, take it further, faster, masters
of their own devices, slow at last
and sway, carried away on your behalf.

Meanwhile, your face is waiting for a bus.
The furthest you might go's a single glance
towards the door, at some hotshot who's just
strolling in, a quick nod to the singer.
I wonder whether they're really your fingers,

which scurry, whir, near and far, which are
a party or a blur. Yet when you're done
and chatting with a guest or a musician,
I watch that same calm face, and your right hand
that's drumming on the bar, that's rattling change.

Jonathan Edwards

The Concert

No, I will go alone.
I will come back when it's over.
Yes, of course I love you.
No, it will not be long.
Why may you not come with me?—
You are too much my lover.
You would put yourself
Between me and song.

If I go alone,
Quiet and suavely clothed,
My body will die in its chair,
And over my head a flame,
A mind that is twice my own,
Will mark with icy mirth
The wise advance and retreat
Of armies without a country,
Storming a nameless gate,
Hurling terrible javelins down
From the shouting walls of a singing town
Where no women wait!
Armies clean of love and hate,
Marching lines of pitiless sound
Climbing hills to the sun and hurling
Golden spears to the ground!
Up the lines a silver runner
Bearing a banner whereon is scored
The milk and steel of a bloodless wound
Healed at length by the sword!

You and I have nothing to do with music.
We may not make of music a filigree frame,
Within which you and I,
Tenderly glad we came,
Sit smiling, hand in hand.

Come now, be content.
I will come back to you, I swear I will;
And you will know me still.
I shall be only a little taller
Than when I went.

Edna St Vincent Millay (1892 – 1950)

The Reed Flute and I
after Mawlana Jalaluddin Rumi

As the reed flute sings you weep your sorrow;
your heart still beats in the place you left. The weight
of your yesterdays that were once tomorrows
halves you, just like the day the reed was cut
pulled from its bed, carved to carry the breath
of the carver to ears held far. Its inhale
is your exhale; as if straight from your own chest.
Its wails redden your eyes. Its larynx speaks your exile.

The same parting that split the reed from its bed
brings you together and you can't know until
you've always known; when they said farewell, you bled
so long, knowing you would not fare well, and still
only long for the place your heart comes from.
Reading in tongues; all music yearns for home.

Abeer Ameer

Song

My father is in the kitchen
making a morning
cup of tea, singing a song
he first heard
when he was a schoolboy,
when both he and Pakistan
were full of possibility.

He claims his memory
is failing, but the song rolls off
his tongue
with such ease I can't help
imagine him suddenly transported
back in time
when Indian films
could ignore history and dwell
on simpler things,
like love.

When my father's song
goes quiet, I pretend his silence
is due to forgetfulness.
I fail to realize
that his eyes have fallen
through the dark
bubbling surface of the tea
and found
for just a moment
the face of his father,
a man who long ago taught
my father this song,
sang it every morning
until the day he disappeared.

Faisal Mohyuddin

The Third Lesson
from Johann Joachim Quantz's Five Lessons

Karl, you are late. The traverse flute is not
A study to take lightly. I am cold waiting.
Put one piece of coal in the stove. This lesson
Shall not be prolonged. Right. Stand in your place.

Ready? Blow me a little ladder of sound
From a good stance so that you feel the heavy
Press of the floor coming up through you and
Keeping your pitch and tone in character.

Now that is something, Karl. You are getting on.
Unswell your head. One more piece of coal.
Go on now but remember it must be always
Easy and flowing. Light and shadow must
Be varied but be varied in your mind
Before you hear the eventual return sound.

Play me the dance you made for the barge-master.
Stop stop Karl. Play it as you first thought
Of it in the hot boat-kitchen. That is a pleasure
For me. I can see I am making you good.
Keep the stove red. Hand me the matches. Now
We can see better. Give me a shot at the pipe.
Karl, I can still put on a good flute-mouth
And show you in this high cold room something
You will be famous to have said you heard.

WS Graham (1918 – 1986)

183

I've heard an Organ talk, sometimes –
In a Cathedral Aisle,
And understood no word it said –
Yet held my breath, the while –

And risen up – and gone away,
A more Bernardine Girl –
Yet – knew not what was done to me
In that old Chapel Aisle.

Emily Dickinson (1830 – 1886)

Guitar

After Lorca's 'Guitarra'

The guitar of California,
of its deserts,
rarely weeps.
Like the cactus, it
conserves its moisture.
Still the guitar breaks
the broad pink bands
of sunset into night,
into a black blued
by the presence of stars.
The guitar cries
without tears into
the night, and the coyote
answers, sometimes
returning the music
note for note.
The guitar cries
for and against
the sky's
impossible breadth.
It calls to
the red-tailed hawk
in his easy sleep.
It calls to the cottontail
whose ears twitch
at the sound.
It cries but releases
no tears: imagine
the weight
of such a heart.

Carrie Etter

from The Princess: The Splendour Falls on Castle Walls

The splendour falls on castle walls
        And snowy summits old in story:
      The long light shakes across the lakes,
        And the wild cataract leaps in glory.
Blow, bugle, blow, set the wild echoes flying,
Blow, bugle; answer, echoes, dying, dying, dying.

      O hark, O hear! how thin and clear,
        And thinner, clearer, farther going!
      O sweet and far from cliff and scar
        The horns of Elfland faintly blowing!
Blow, let us hear the purple glens replying:
Blow, bugle; answer, echoes, dying, dying, dying.

      O love, they die in yon rich sky,
        They faint on hill or field or river:
      Our echoes roll from soul to soul,
        And grow for ever and for ever.
Blow, bugle, blow, set the wild echoes flying,
And answer, echoes, answer, dying, dying, dying.

Alfred Lord Tennyson (1809 – 1892)

The Trumpeter

O trumpeter, methinks I am myself the instrument thou playest
Thou melt'st my heart, my brain—thou movest, drawest, chan-
gest them at will
                    The Mystic Trumpeter
                    Walt Whitman

I have seen the trumpeter, the *bright wolf*
crossing over the mountain stream,
their trumpet flashing silver
like some half-remembered dream.

I have seen their breath hanging
in frost-bitten air as they climbed
a staircase dressed in shadows,
set amongst the trees and outlined

dark against the bluest light,
saw how each step was balanced
in the air but led to nowhere.
The sound they left behind

was a sound so full of distance,
an echo of an echo caught
by fallen leaves, a half-finished
phrase, like a passing thought

just waiting for an answer.
They hold the horn against
their lips. And now it feels as if
their hands are on my waist,

their fingers resting light
as knowing. My body turns
to metal beneath their touch.
Life is cold. Their breath burns

through the heart of me.
Oh I am all hollow and resistance,
all silence and astonishment.
This is my new existence,

so blow one clear note through me,
here in the field laced with water.
Hold me close as I transform.
I'll answer questions later.

Kim Moore

Étudier
(for Miss Forbes and Sharon Cranmer)

I played the beautiful music of the dead –
waltzes, *études*. Miss Forbes would hold her pencil
and make the faintest marks in her 2B lead.
So particular, her parlour with its sills
of old cracked china and dried camellias.
She said, *if only you would practise more*
and when I did, my hands would sing across
the keys. With her, I learnt what learning was for.

She died. I went to Sharon, who wore black –
embroidered skirts, black lipstick, blue-black hair –
her thin, mercurial hands. In the room upstairs,
I played Debussy – better than before –
but my eye was on the albums leant in stacks
beside the door, *The Smiths, The Clash, The Cure.*

Hannah Lowe